THE HIP-HOP REVOLUTION

DRAKE
ACTING AND RAPPING TO THE TOP

BARBARA
GOTTFRIED

Enslow Publishing

101 W. 23rd Street
Suite 240
New York, NY 10011
USA
enslow.com

This book is dedicated to Lauren Garrett, a very big Drake fan. Lauren makes such an incredible difference in this world with her kindness.

Published in 2020 by Enslow Publishing, LLC.
101 W. 23rd Street, Suite 240, New York, NY 10011

Library of Congress Cataloging-in-Publication Data
Names: Gottfried, Barbara, author.
Title: Drake : acting and rapping to the top / Barbara Gottfried.
Description: New York, NY : Enslow Publishing, LLC., 2020. | Series: The hip-hop revolution | Audience: 5 | Includes bibliographical references and index.
Identifiers: LCCN 2018046438| ISBN 9781978509658 (library bound) | ISBN 9781978510104 (pbk.) | ISBN 9781978510128 (6 pack)
Subjects: LCSH: Drake, 1986—Juvenile literature. | Rap musicians—Canada—Biography—Juvenile literature. | Actors—Canada—Biography—Juvenile literature.
Classification: LCC ML3930.D73 D72 2018 | DDC 782.421649092 [B] —dc23
LC record available at https://lccn.loc.gov/2018046438

Printed in the United States of America

To Our Readers: We have done our best to make sure all websites in this book were active and appropriate when we went to press. However, the author and the publisher have no control over and assume no liability for the material available on those websites or on any websites they may link to. Any comments or suggestions can be sent by email to customerservice@enslow.com.

Photo Credits: Cover, pp. 1, 17, 23 Ethan Miller/WireImage/Getty Images; p. 5 Skip Bolen/WireImage/Getty Images; pp. 7, 8 George Pimentel/WireImage/Getty Images; p. 11 Thaddaeus McAdams/WireImage/Getty Images; p. 12 Kathy Hutchins/Shutterstock.com; p. 14 © AP Images; p. 18 Johnny Nunez/WireImage/Getty Images; p. 21 Prince Williams/WireImage/Getty Images; p. 25 Justin Sullivan/Getty Images; p. 27 Splash News/Lotus House/Newscom; title graphics (arrows) Vecster/Shutterstock.com.

CONTENTS

THE BEGINNING OF A RAPPER

Drake is now a successful rapper. But his early life was not easy. Aubrey Drake Graham was born on October 24, 1986, in Toronto, Canada. Drake's father, Dennis, was a drummer. His mother, Sandi, was an English teacher. His dad is Catholic and African American, and his mom is white and Jewish Canadian.

"Nobody understood what it was like to be black and Jewish," said Drake. "Being different from everyone else just made me a lot stronger."[1]

When Drake was five years old, his parents divorced. His dad moved to Tennessee, and Drake stayed with his mom in Toronto.

Drake grew up on Weston Road in Toronto until the end of sixth grade. In this neighborhood, people struggled to pay the bills. Drake's mom worked hard,

but they did not have a lot of money. Later, Drake and his mom moved to a wealthier part of Toronto called Forest Hills. This part had mansions, but Drake and his mom rented the basement and first floor of someone's home.

Special Times

When Drake was thirteen years old, he had a Jewish ceremony called a bar mitzvah. Later, when Drake turned thirty-one years old, he had a re-bar mitzvah party. Some people think Drake chose the age thirty-one because it is the reverse of thirteen.

GOING TO WORK

When Drake was about fourteen, his dad, Dennis Graham, was in prison. Graham shared a jail cell with a man named Poverty who liked to rap. During Drake's phone calls with Dennis, Poverty encouraged Drake to start rapping. Rap is a kind of music with words set to rhythm and a beat. Drake and Poverty shared their raps over the phone.

Drake attended two high schools called Forest Hill Collegiate and Vaughan Road Academy. Some students at Vaughan Road Academy bullied Drake for being Jewish and biracial. During this time, Drake's mother was sick, and they still did not have much money. Drake wanted to help by working, but he went to school all day. At the age of fifteen, Drake quit high school. He hoped to earn money by acting full-time.

"One of the greatest feelings in my entire life. As of tonight, I have graduated high school!"[2]

Drake's mother was a teacher. She was not happy when Drake quit school. Drake promised his mom that he would finish high school someday. The University of

Drake poses with his mother, Sandi Graham, at the Juno Awards on March 27, 2011, in Toronto, Canada. Drake and his mother share a close relationship.

Kentucky basketball coach, named John Calipari, also inspired Drake to finish school. He kept his promise to his mother. At twenty-five years old, Drake earned his high school diploma. He also gave the graduation speech at Jarvis Collegiate Institute in Toronto in 2012.

Drake costars with Shane Kippel (*right*) on the one hundredth episode of *Degrassi: The Next Generation*. The show was filmed in Drake's hometown of Toronto, Canada.

CHOOSING MUSIC

At the age of fifteen, Drake began acting on a TV show called *Degrassi: The Next Generation*. In 2012, the show became the longest-running Canadian series. *Degrassi* explored challenging teen issues, with each character reacting differently to them. Drake played a character named Jimmy Brooks. He was a basketball player.

On *Degrassi,* Drake's character was called Brooks. In one episode, Brooks was shot by another student named Rick Murray. Brooks became paralyzed from the waist down and had to use a wheelchair to get around. During another episode, the character Ashley Kerwin performs in a school talent contest. Brooks joins her and raps from his wheelchair.

Drake tried to balance both acting and music. He spent all day on the *Degrassi* set. After work, Drake made music in a studio. Sometimes, Drake would play music until five o'clock in the morning and still begin work on *Degrassi* at nine o'clock. Eventually, Drake had to choose between acting and music. He chose music.

However, Drake did not forget his former costars. *Degrassi: The Next Generation,* ended in 2015. But the cast from the show had a reunion in a music video for Drake's song "I'm Upset." The video included Drake and more than twenty people from the show. "I'm Upset" is part of Drake's 2018 album, *Scorpion.*

IT'S A RAP

Drake's dad played the drums. Drake's uncle Larry played a string instrument called a bass. Music was in Drake's family. Drake's first mixtape was *Room for Improvement*. It featured two other music artists, Trey Songz and Lupe Fiasco. More than six thousand copies sold. Drake's second mixtape was called *Comeback Season*. It had the hit song "Replacement Girl," which appeared

Ways to Listen

Both albums and mixtapes can include songs or remixes. Albums cost money to buy, but mixtapes are usually free. *So Far Gone* could be downloaded for free at Drake's site, called October's Very Own.

on the Black Entertainment Television (BET) channel with a music video.

Drake's third mixtape made it huge. *So Far Gone* had the hit singles "Best I Ever Had" and "Successful." Both songs received gold certification, which means they were downloaded more than five hundred thousand times. "Best I Ever Had" even made it to number two on the Billboard Hot 100 chart. After *So Far Gone*, record companies competed to sign Drake for an album. Drake chose rapper Lil Wayne's record company, called Young Money Entertainment.

Drake's dad, Dennis Graham, joined Drake for the 2016 Summer Sixteen tour. Graham is an R&B singer and social media celebrity.

Drake appears at the 55th Annual Grammy Awards in Los Angeles, California, on February 10, 2013. Drake won his first Grammy at this ceremony.

WINNING AWARDS AND TOURING THE WORLD

After signing with the record company, Drake released his first studio album, *Thank Me Later*. His album went platinum that same month, which means it sold one million copies. In 2010, Drake also went on the Away From Home tour. He performed on fifteen college campuses. The shows also featured college groups that shared ways to keep the environment healthy. The Away From Home tour was later extended to other parts of the United States, Canada, and Europe.

In 2010, Drake also hosted his first OVO Fest, featuring famous rappers Jay-Z and Eminem. In 2015, he played his hit song "Hotline Bling" for the first time at OVO Fest. Today, OVO Fest is still an annual concert that Drake holds in Toronto with many other famous performers.

After *Thank Me Later*, Drake had another album, *Take Care*. Before an album comes out, some of the album's songs are released on the radio or made available for download. If the songs are popular, then more people will buy the album when it comes out. Three songs from *Take Care* were released before the album, and they all became popular. *Take Care* won Best Rap Album at the 55th Annual Grammy Awards.

The album *Take Care* also helped Drake win an MTV award for Best Hip-Hop Video. Drake's *Take Care* is an example of an emo album. Emo rap is a kind of music with lyrics that express emotion. In some of the lyrics from the songs in *Take Care*, Drake examines the meaning of success and shares some of his ideas on romance.

In 2011, Drake signed autographs in Toronto before his album *Take Care* came out. *Take Care* spent more than 250 weeks on the Billboard 200 music chart.

He explores the struggle between wanting and having and between imagination and reality.

ARTSY ALBUM COVERS

The cover of *Take Care* shows a sad Drake, alone and deep in thought. According to Drake, it depicts the transformation of a "kid that's just somehow gone from his mom's basement in Toronto to becoming a king."[1] Following *Take Care*, Drake did the Club Paradise tour. The tour had sixty-seven shows and made more money than any hip-hop tour in 2012.

"Sometimes, it's the journey that teaches you a lot about your destination."[2]

The next year, Drake released his third album, called *Nothing Was the Same*. The cover art of this album is an oil painting by artist Kadir Nelson. It shows Drake as a baby on one side and Drake as an adult on the other side. These images represent his past and his present.

KEEP IT COMING

Drake kept turning out top albums. His next one was called *Views*. It was based on the change of seasons in Toronto. Drake really got to work on the album in the fall of 2015. He stayed in Toronto during the winter to record the album's section about this cold season. *Views* is dedicated to Megan Flores, who was a terminally ill cancer patient. Megan had asked the Make-a-Wish Foundation for one wish—to meet her favorite singer, Drake. He granted her wish. In 2016, Megan died at the age of fourteen. Drake posted a tribute that included, "I am blessed to have known you in this lifetime."[1]

Views was a huge success. In 2017, Drake won thirteen awards at the Billboard Music Awards. His wins were largely due to *Views* and a hit song from that album called "One Dance." Among the awards, Drake won Top Artist,

Drake wins a Top Billboard Album Award for *Views* on May 21, 2017, in Las Vegas, Nevada. The album was originally named *View from the 6*, referring to Toronto.

Top Hot 100 Artist, Top Billboard 200 Album, and Top Billboard 200 Artist. In 2016, "One Dance" topped the Hot 100 chart for ten weeks. It was also the first song to get one billion plays on the music-streaming service Spotify. Drake sang on "One Dance" with two other music artists, Kyla and Wizkid.

ANOTHER HIT ALBUM

Drake's next album, *More Life*, was released in 2017. Kanye West was a coproducer on this album. It includes twenty-two songs. *More Life* got more than one billion streams in the United States. The album was streamed on services such as Apple Music, Amazon, and Spotify, but it was announced on Drake's own OVO Sound Radio.

Drake and PartyNextDoor pose for a photo at the Sound of Brazil on October 23, 2014. PartyNextDoor is a fellow Canadian rapper.

Drake called *More Life* "a playlist" because he wanted many artists to work on this music project in different ways.[2] It features many musicians, including Kanye West, Lil Wayne, Young Thug, and PartyNextDoor. The album's song "Glow" was created with eighteen artists, songwriters, and producers.

In *More Life*, Drake also brings together different countries. "Glow" was produced by South African DJ Black Coffee. The song "Madiba Riddim" mentions former South African leader Nelson Mandela. This album also includes beats from a type of popular Jamaican music called dancehall. Even the name *More Life* comes from a Jamaican slang phrase that means "to wish someone well."[3]

Hoops and Rap

Drake loves basketball. Some of the songs on *More Life* mention several basketball stars, such as Kevin Durant, Kobe Bryant, and Michael Jordan. Drake also attends many basketball games. He cheers for the Toronto Raptors.

SONGS OF TRUTH

In 2018, Drake continued his success story with his next album, *Scorpion*. Drake's albums are like a personal journey. He sings about his childhood, becoming a famous rapper, his relationships, his thoughts on life . . . and finally, in *Scorpion*, himself today. This album even mentions someone that Drake kept private until the album's release—his son, Adonis. He was born October 11, 2017. The songs "Emotionless," "8 out of 10," and "March 14" mention being a single dad and wanting to hide the world from his son. On this album, Drake also shares thoughts on the harmful side of social media and his feuds with other rappers. *Scorpion* even includes a song for his mom called "Sandra's Rose."

"Live without pretending, Love without depending, Listen without defending, Speak without offending."[4]

Scorpion is a double album featuring two types of music separately. Side A has rap and side B has R&B (or rhythm and blues). This album was the first during this century to have a record seven Hot 100 Top 10

Drake performs on the 2018 Aubrey & The Three Amigos tour in Chicago, Illinois. The tour included forty-one performance dates and celebrated Drake's album *Scorpion*.

songs. These songs include "God's Plan," "Nonstop," "I'm Upset," and "Emotionless" from side A. "Nice for What," "In My Feelings," and "Don't Matter to Me" come from side B. From all his mixtapes and albums, Drake has had thirty-one top ten hits. He beat famous singer Michael Jackson's record.

4

DOING BUSINESS AND GIVING BACK

Drake has a company called OVO. "OVO" Stands for "October's Very Own." Drake and his crew all have October birthdays. Written as "OvO," an owl appears with two eyes and a beak in the middle. The owl is the company's logo.

In 2012, Drake and friends Noah "40" Shebib and Oliver El-Khatib founded OVO SOUND. This record label produces and sells music from musicians such as PartyNextDoor, Majid Jordan, and Baka Not Nice. It also sells clothing featuring its artists, including T-shirts, tanks, sweatshirts, and hats.

In 2011, OVO launched its own clothing line. Drake worked with the big Canadian clothing brand Roots to sell jackets. Drake also partnered with a store called Colette in Paris, France, and another called Browns in London, England.

OTHER BUSINESS VENTURES

Drake's musical success has earned him millions. But he also earns money in other ways. The OVO company makes about $4.3 million a year.[1] Drake also earns money by having part ownership in companies. He has invested in both Virginia Black Whiskey and the Toronto Raptors NBA team.

Drake is paid by companies to endorse, or publicly support, their products. Companies hope people will buy the same products that Drake uses. For example,

Drake gives a concert at the Hard Rock Hotel and Casino on January 1, 2012, in Las Vegas, Nevada. The OVO logo glows in the background.

Drake signed a deal with Apple worth $19 million to use its products.[2] And Drake has endorsed clothing, such Nike's Jordan brand. He has also appeared in commercials for the popular drink Sprite as part of its "Spark" campaign.

The "Spark" campaign included an ad called "Unleashed." This ad begins with Drake looking for inspiration to record the hit song "Forever." Drake has a Sprite, and the drink goes through his body, finding its way to his speaker-shaped heart. This ad campaign also had a film project that allowed people to edit their own forty-five-second animated films. Sprite hoped to show that its drink sparks creativity.

Blogs and Fests

The first OVO blogs shared Drake's thoughts about music, relationships, and life. Today this blog is more about sharing songs, videos, and pictures. In 2010, Drake launched the first OVO Fest in Toronto. It is now one of the most talked about music festivals. It features different popular musicians each year—including Drake.

Drake and Apple's senior vice president Eddy Cue give each other high fives at an Apple conference in San Francisco, California. Drake wears a jacket with the Apple logo.

HELPING OTHERS

Drake grew up with a single mom who struggled to pay the bills. Now he is very wealthy from his music, ads, and investments. Drake also believes in giving back. He donates money to those in need.

For example, in 2010, Drake gave money to the Jamaican Learning Center to build computer schools. In 2011, he gave to Dixon Hall in Toronto, which helps those living in poor neighborhoods. Drake aided a shelter by giving charity to Portland's Union Gospel Mission in 2013. That year, Drake also gave to a mother from Ohio who lost her children and husband to a home fire. Drake's charitable donations have also included the 2017 Hurricane Harvey relief efforts to help Houston victims of that storm.

> "I like it when money makes a difference, but don't make you different."[3]

During the first half of 2018, Drake gave away almost $1 million to homeless children, college kids, and others in Miami.[4] Those who received this charity included Miami Senior High School, the Miami Fire Department,

DATE 02/06/18   004

PAY TO THE
ORDER OF Lotus House Women's Shelter $ 50,000.00

Fifty Thousand---------------------------------------00/100 DOLLARS

MEMO Donation

⑆3332667687⑆   7867041401⑈   004

Drake donates $50,000 to Lotus House Women's Shelter on February 8, 2018, in Miami, Florida, as well as toys and gift cards.

and the Lotus House homeless shelter. Drake's donations appeared in his video for the single "God's Plan." Drake continues to use his fame and wealth to improve the lives of those less fortunate.

TIMELINE

1986 Aubrey Drake Graham is born October 24 in Toronto, Canada.

1999 Drake has his bar mitzvah at the age of thirteen.

2001 Drake first appears on *Degrassi: The Next Generation*.

2006 Drake releases his first mixtape, *Room for Improvement*.

2010 Drake releases his first album, *Thank Me Later*.

2010 OVO Fest premieres in Toronto, Canada.

2013 *Take Care* wins Drake a Grammy for Best Rap Album.

2013 Drake becomes global ambassador for the Toronto Raptors basketball team.

2017 *More Life* gets more than one billion streams in the United States in April.

2017 Drake wins thirteen Billboard Music Awards.

2017 Drake's son, Adonis, is born October 11.

2018 Drake releases his double album, *Scorpion*.

2018 Drake gives away almost $1 million to help those in need.

CHAPTER NOTES

CHAPTER 1. THE BEGINNING OF A RAPPER

1. Allison Simon, "Drake," Arrowhead, January 25, 2014, https://whrhsarrowhead.com/2816/uncategorized/drake/.

2. Gil Kaufman, "Rapper Finally Graduated from High School After Dropping Out to Be in 'Degrassi,'" MTV News, October 18, 2012, http://www.mtv.com/news/1695780/drake-high-school-diploma/.

CHAPTER 2. IT'S A RAP

1. Rob Markman, "Drake Finds 'King' Crown Heavy on *Take Care*," MTV News, October 17, 2011, http://www.mtv.com/news/1672619/drake-take-care-album-cover/.

2. "Drake Gives High School Graduation Speech," Rap-Up, October 27, 2012, https://www.rap-up.com/2012/10/27/drake-gives-high-school-graduation-speech/.

CHAPTER 3. KEEP IT COMING

1. Sandra Song, "Drake and Rihanna Post Touching Tributes to a Young Fan Who Passed Away," *Paper*, July 11, 2016, http://www.papermag.com/drake-rihanna-1915996148.html.

2. HP Cheung, "10 Things You Should Know About Drake's 'More Life,'" Hypebeast, March 20, 2017, https://hypebeast.com/2017/3/drake-more-life-album-facts-things-to-know.

3. Ibid.

4. Drake (@Drake), "Live without pretending, Love without depending, Listen without defending, Speak without offending," Twitter, February 20, 2011, 10:14 p.m., https://twitter.com/drake/status/39568541719986176.

CHAPTER 4. DOING BUSINESS AND GIVING BACK

1. Samantha McDonald, "Drake's Net Worth: Started from the Bottom, Now He's Worth a Fortune," FN, August 3, 2018, https://footwearnews.com/2018/focus/entertainment/drake-net-worth-1202647143/.

2. Ibid.

3. "30 Drake Lyrics That Will Give You All the Feels," Capital Xtra, https://www.capitalxtra.com/artists/drake/lists/emotional-lyrics/ (accessed September 24, 2018).

4. Chabeli Herrera, "Drake Had Almost $1 Million to Spend on a Music Video. He Gave It All to Miami," *Miami Herald*, February 16, 2018, https://www.miamiherald.com/entertainment/article200517604.html.

GLOSSARY

ad campaign A series of advertisements with one idea or product.

biracial Being of two different races.

brand The symbol or name used by a company to sell its products.

charity Something, such as money, given to people who need it.

creativity The ability to use imagination to create something, such as art.

donation Something given away, such as money.

endorse To openly support something in public.

mixtape A collection of songs recorded by rappers and DJs, usually either given away for free or sold at a low cost.

rap A kind of music with fast words said to rhythm and with instruments behind it.

rhythm A pattern of sounds, musical notes, and words.

rhythm and blues (R&B) A type of popular music invented by African Americans with blues and jazz elements.

Spotify A streaming music service.

FURTHER READING

BOOKS

Burling, Alexis. *Drake: Hip-Hop Superstar.* Minneapolis, MN: Essential Library, 2018.

Isbell, Hannah. *Drake: Actor and Rapper.* New York, NY: Enslow Publishing, 2017.

Snellgrove, Chris. *Drake.* Broomall, PA: Mason Crest, 2019.

WEBSITES

Drake
drakeofficial.com
Visit Drake's official website for music, videos, tour dates, merchandise, and more.

Kidzworld
www.kidzworld.com/article/5321-pioneers-of-hip-hop
Find out how hip-hop and rap got started.

INDEX